Success
Learn and Practise

Maths
age 7-8

YEAR
3

Paul Broadbent

Contents

Using and applying mathematics

Counting and understanding numbers

Knowing and using number facts

Calculating

Understanding shape

Measuring

Handling data

Knowing and using number facts

Glossary

Answers

Problem-solving

Read word problems carefully to work out the calculations that are needed. Always follow these four easy steps:

Step 1: Read the problem.

Try to picture the problem and imagine going through it in real life.

Step 2: Sort out the calculations.

You might need to add, subtract, multiply or divide. Sometimes more than one calculation is needed.

Step 3: Answer the calculations.

Work out the answers carefully.

Step 4: Answer the problem.

Look back at the question – what is it asking?

Exercise 1

Answer these problems.

a A candle is 26cm long. It burns down 18cm.
   How long is it now?   _____

b Josh has 90 stamps in his collection and is given another
   10 by his aunt. How many stamps are there altogether?   _____

c Eve had 12 friends and 7 relatives at her party.
   How many people did Eve invite to her party in total?   _____

d Mrs French has 70p and spends 25p on a newspaper.
   How much money has she got left?   _____

e Kate is 10, her mother is 40 and her gran is 70.
   What is their total age?   _____

f How old was Gran when Kate was born?   _____

Exercise 2

Answer these.

a At the school cake stall Mr Green buys 5 biscuits at 9p each and 2 cakes that cost 30p each. What is the total cost of Mr Green's biscuits and cakes? _____

b There are 6 eggs in a box. 5 full egg boxes have been dropped and 8 eggs are broken. How many eggs are left? _____

c Gina collected 25 conkers, Ali collected 20 and Matt collected 15. They put all the conkers together and shared them equally. How many conkers did they each get? _____

d Mrs Khan bought a book for £4, a pen for £3 and a CD for £12. How much change did she get from £20? _____

e These are the ingredients to make 10 currant buns. 120g flour, 40g sugar, 30g butter, 60g egg, 50g currants. How much will each bun weigh? _____

Challenge

Make up your own maths problem, by writing down any calculation, such as 12 + 6 = 18. Then make up a word problem for this calculation.

For example: An elephant stored 12 nuts at the top of a tree and 6 more at the bottom. How many nuts did he store altogether?

Try this for different calculations.

Brain Teaser

Try these 'think of a number' problems:

1 I think of a number, then add 5.
The answer is 13. What was my number? ☐

2 I think of a number, then subtract 11.
The answer is 17. What was my number? ☐

3 I think of a number, then multiply by 3.
The answer is 21. What was my number? ☐

Money

These are the coins and notes that we use.

There are 100 pence in £1. We use a **decimal point** to show the pounds and the pence: £1.85.

£2.50 = 250p £5.00 = 500p £3.25 = 325p

Exercise 1

Total each amount.   50+10+5

a

£ 1.22

b

[　　　] p

c

£ [　　　]

d

[　　　] p

Exercise 2

What is the change from £2 for each of these?

a £1.30 [　] 　　b 90p [　] 　　c £1.05 [　]

d £1.75 [　] 　　e 40p [　] 　　f 75p [　]

Exercise 3

Look at the picture and then answer the questions.

WORLD OF PETS

bottle £1.15
wheel £4.50
ball £3.75
food 82p
cage £8

a How much would two bags of food cost?

b What is the total cost of a cage, water bottle and exercise wheel?

c How much change would you get from £5 if you bought the exercise ball?

d How much more is the wheel than the exercise ball?

e Harry has 4 coins. It is exactly enough money to buy a bag of food. What are the four coins Harry has? Draw them in this wallet.

 Top Tip To work out an amount of change, count on from the cost of the item to the amount given.

If something costs £1.65, the change from £2 is 35p.

5p   10p   20p

£1.65 £1.70 £1.80 £2.00

Challenge

Grab a shopping catalogue and see if you can use it to reach target amounts. For example, give yourself a target of £20 to spend. Choose a page and try to estimate spending just under £20 on different numbers of items. Check your estimate with a calculator. If you go over £20 you lose – if you are close to £20 you win. The target can be changed to £50. Why don't you have a go?

Brain Teaser

Use five coins to make these different amounts.

1 £1.36 ◯◯◯◯◯

2 £2.67 ◯◯◯◯◯

3 94p ◯◯◯◯◯

4 £3.13 ◯◯◯◯◯

Number sequences

Number **sequences** are patterns of numbers with the same-sized steps.

Sequences can go up:

3 5 7 9 …

40 50 60 70 …

or down:

900 800 700 600 …

34 32 30 28 …

To work out missing numbers in sequences, look at the **difference** between each number.

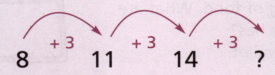

8   +3   11   +3   14   +3   ?

The next number is 17.

Exercise 1

Write the next three numbers in each of these sequences.

a 27   29   31   33   ☐ ☐ ☐

b 80   78   76   74   ☐ ☐ ☐

c 42   52   62   72   ☐ ☐ ☐

d 112   212   312   412   ☐ ☐ ☐

e 96   86   76   66   ☐ ☐ ☐

f 168   158   148   138   ☐ ☐ ☐

Exercise 2

Write the missing numbers in each of these sequences.

a   9   —13   17   ☐   ☐   29   ☐   37

b   31   28   ☐   22   19   16   ☐   ☐

c   6   11   ☐   21   26   ☐   ☐   41

d   54   ☐   46   42   38   ☐   ☐   26

Exercise 3

Circle the even numbers in these number lines.

a   137   138   139   140   141   142

b   240   239   238   237   236   235

c   809   810   811   812   813   814   815   816

 Odd numbers end in 1, 3, 5, 7 and 9.

Even numbers end in 0, 2, 4, 6 and 8.

Challenge

A fun way to learn about number sequences is to look at car registration plates and try to spot any three numbers that show a sequence.

For example: T147 RFW has a +3 sequence: 1 (+3) 4 (+3) 7

Next time you're in the car, why don't you have a go?

Brain Teaser

Number sequences can include negative numbers. Write the missing numbers on these number lines.

1   ☐   ☐   −2   −1   0   1   ☐

2   −3   ☐   ☐   ☐   1   2   ☐

Three-digit numbers

Numbers are made from the ten **digits**:

$$0 \ 1 \ 2 \ 3 \ 4 \ 5 \ 6 \ 7 \ 8 \ 9$$

The important thing to remember is that the position of a digit in a number gives its value.

$$458 = 400 + 50 + 8$$

hundreds   tens   ones

To multiply by 10 move all the digits one place to the left.

The empty place is filled by a zero.

$$38 \times 10 =$$

3 8 0

To divide by 10 move all the digits one place to the right.

$$490 \div 10 =$$

4 9

Exercise 1

Join the numbers to the words.

six hundred and ninety-four

three hundred and sixty-eight

one hundred and twenty-four

680

368

964

683

694

124

six hundred and eighty

nine hundred and sixty-four

six hundred and eighty-three

Exercise 2

Write the missing numbers.

a $495 = 400 + \boxed{} + 5$

b $538 = \boxed{} + \boxed{} + \boxed{}$

c $746 = \boxed{} + \boxed{} + \boxed{}$

d $734 = \boxed{} + \boxed{} + \boxed{}$

e $849 = \boxed{} + \boxed{} + \boxed{}$

f $293 = \boxed{} + \boxed{} + \boxed{}$

Exercise 3

Write the numbers coming out of each machine.

a 68

42

 **IN** × 10 **OUT**

81

90

b 320

400

IN ÷ 10 **OUT**

740

680

 Top Tip *Zero is a very important digit. It is easy to confuse the numbers 204, 240, 2040 and 2400. For numbers like these, look carefully at the position of the zeros.*

Challenge

Playing Digit Boxes is fun on your own or with a friend. Use digit cards 0-9 shuffled and placed face down.

Draw three boxes and then turn over the top card. Write the digit in one of the boxes, with the aim to make the largest 3-digit number possible.

Once the digit is written, repeat this twice more until the 3-digit number is complete. Is it the largest number possible? Try it with 4-digit numbers.

Brain Teaser

Which number is each arrow pointing to?

1

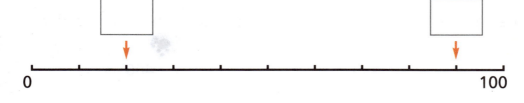

2

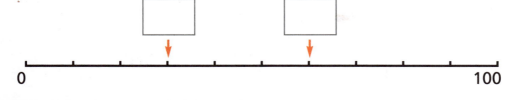

Comparing and ordering

When you need to **compare** numbers to find the largest or smallest, it is helpful to write them under each other, lining up the units.

For example: Josh scored 748 points on a computer game, and Emma scored 780. Who got the highest score?

Line them up:

hundreds	tens	ones
7	4	8
7	8	0

Compare the hundreds, tens and ones and you can see that 780 is bigger because it has 8 tens.

You can use the same method to put a set of numbers in order of size.

Put these in order starting with the smallest:

154   290   406   298

Line them up and put them in order:

hundreds	tens	ones
1	5	4
2	9	0
2	9	8
4	0	6

Exercise 1

Circle the smallest number in each pair.

a 412   242   **b** 606   660   **c** 594   592   **d** 800   796

Exercise 2

Write a number on each card so that the five numbers are in size order.

a 384   ☐   399   ☐   406

b ☐   615   ☐   637   648

c 825   ☐   ☐   878   891

Exercise 3

Write these amounts in order, starting with the smallest.

a | 714ml 284ml 842ml 738ml 480ml

_____ _____ _____ _____ _____

b | 856g 865g 560g 681g 650g

_____ _____ _____ _____ _____

Exercise 4

Join these numbers to their correct positions.

381   337   314   373   356

300 |————————————————————————————————| 400

 Top Tip *Remember to read each number from the left to the right. Compare all the hundreds first and put them in order, then the tens, and finally the ones.*

Challenge

Use digit cards 0–9. Pick out any four cards and make as many different 3-digit numbers as you can. Write them in order, starting with the smallest.

How many different 3-digit numbers can you make? How many 2-digit or 4-digit numbers can you make? Try it with different sets of digits.

Brain Teaser

Each of these should be in order. Colour the two numbers that have been swapped in each row.

1 | 214 | 215 | 219 | 217 | 218 | 216

2 | 375 | 370 | 373 | 372 | 371 | 374

3 | 684 | 682 | 683 | 681 | 685 | 686

Rounding numbers

Rounding makes numbers easier to work with – changing them to the nearest ten or hundred.

Rounding to the nearest 10.

- Look at the ones digit.
- If it is 5 or more, round up the tens digit.
- If it is less than 5, the tens digit stays the same.

35 rounds up to 40.

64 rounds down to 60.

30   35   40   60   64   70

Rounding to the nearest 100.

- Look at the tens digits.
- If it is 50 or more, round up the hundreds digit.
- If it is less than 50, the hundreds digit stays the same.

763 rounds up to 800.

537 rounds down to 500.

700   763   800   500   537   600

Exercise 1

Round these numbers to the nearest 10.

a 48 → ☐

b 75 → ☐

c 12 → ☐

d 83 → ☐

e 56 → ☐

f 47 → ☐

g 59 → ☐

h 64 → ☐

i 35 → ☐

Exercise 2

Round these numbers to the nearest 100.

a 317 → ☐

b 184 → ☐

c 210 → ☐

d 264 → ☐

e 706 → ☐

f 638 → ☐

g 548 → ☐

h 850 → ☐

i 192 → ☐

Exercise 3

Join these numbers to the nearest 10.

27   42   58   74   85   96

10   20   30   40   50   60   70   80   90   100

Exercise 4

Write five numbers that you would round to 400 (to the nearest 100).

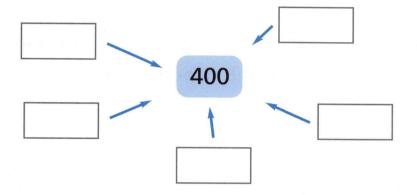

 Top Tip *We round up if the number is halfway between two tens or two hundreds. So, for example, 35 rounds up to 40 and 250 rounds up to 300.*

Challenge

Choose a big book with lots of pages. Make sure you can lift it! Open it up at any page and look at the page number. Work out which number this rounds to, to the nearest 10, and then check by counting on or back through the pages. This is a good way of checking how quick and accurate you are at rounding.

Brain Teaser

Each of these needs rounding to the nearest 100. Circle the correct answer.

1   1428   →   1500   1430   1400

2   3084   →   3000   3100   3090

3   6245   →   6200   6250   6300

Fractions

When you read or write a **fraction**, the bottom part of the fraction, or **denominator**, tells you the number of equal parts.

Look at these:

 → $\frac{1}{2}$ → one half → one whole divided into 2 equal parts

 → $\frac{1}{4}$ → one quarter → one whole divided into 4 equal parts

 → $\frac{1}{10}$ → one tenth → one whole divided into 10 equal parts

To find fractions of amounts, just divide by the denominator.

$\frac{1}{3}$ of 6 is the same as 6 divided by 3, which is 2

Exercise 1

Write the fraction that each shape is shaded.

a [ ]   b [ ]   c [ ]   d [ ]

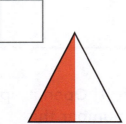   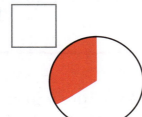   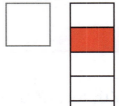   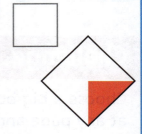

Exercise 2

Colour these shapes to show the fractions.

a $\frac{1}{4}$    b $\frac{1}{5}$ 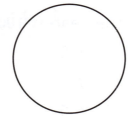   c $\frac{1}{2}$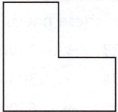

Exercise 3

Draw loops around the sweets to show the fraction. Write the answers.

a $\frac{1}{4}$ of 12 = ☐   **b** $\frac{1}{2}$ of 6 = ☐   **c** $\frac{1}{3}$ of 12 = ☐

Exercise 4

Colour $\frac{1}{4}$ of this flag red. Colour $\frac{1}{2}$ blue.

 Top Tip *The same fraction can look different. All these are the same as a half.*

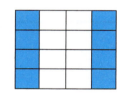
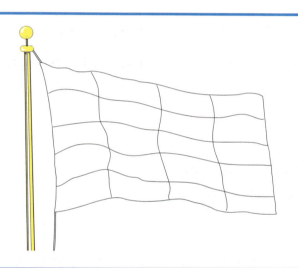

Challenge

You can make half patterns, just draw a square grid of 16 squares. Now shade half of the squares to make a colourful pattern. How many squares will be coloured?

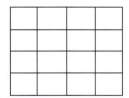

Repeat this on other grids to make different half patterns.

Brain Teaser

What must be added to each of these fractions to make 1?

1 $\frac{1}{2}$ + ☐   **2** $\frac{1}{4}$ + ☐

3 $\frac{2}{3}$ + ☐   **4** $\frac{1}{10}$ + ☐

5 $\frac{7}{10}$ + ☐   **6** $\frac{4}{9}$ + ☐

Addition and subtraction facts

When you add two numbers together, the order in which you add does not matter.

4 + 7 is the same as 7 + 4.

You can start with either number. This means that you have half as many addition facts to remember. If you know the answer to 8 + 4, then you also know the answer to 4 + 8.

When you subtract, the order does matter.

12 − 5 is not the same as 5 − 12.

It is important to know which number you are starting with, so you can then take an amount away from it.

Make sure you know these three signs:

+ is the addition sign   **−** is the subtraction sign

= is the equal sign

Exercise 1

Complete these addition squares.

a

+	4	6	2
7	11		
3			
8			

b

+	6	3	11
5	11		
9			
4			

c

+	6	4	5
12	18		
14			
9			

Exercise 2

Write the difference between each pair of numbers.

a 14   9 ☐

b 8   11 ☐

c 17   14 ☐

d 6   13 ☐

e 15   8 ☐

f 19   13 ☐

Exercise 3

Try to answer each column of sums as quickly as you can.
Time yourself to find your quickest time.

a 7 + 2 = ☐
   5 + 3 = ☐
   2 + 8 = ☐
   4 + 6 = ☐
   3 + 4 = ☐
   2 + 5 = ☐
   6 + 3 = ☐
   4 + 5 = ☐

b 7 + 6 = ☐
   8 + 7 = ☐
   6 + 5 = ☐
   4 + 9 = ☐
   5 + 8 = ☐
   4 + 7 = ☐
   8 + 8 = ☐
   9 + 6 = ☐

c 5 − 2 = ☐
   8 − 6 = ☐
   6 − 1 = ☐
   10 − 3 = ☐
   8 − 4 = ☐
   7 − 3 = ☐
   10 − 5 = ☐
   9 − 8 = ☐

d 18 − 9 = ☐
   11 − 3 = ☐
   14 − 6 = ☐
   12 − 6 = ☐
   17 − 8 = ☐
   16 − 9 = ☐
   12 − 8 = ☐
   11 − 2 = ☐

Top Tip   Use addition facts that you know to help work out subtraction facts.
For example, if you know that 7 + 5 = 12, then you can use this to work out 12 − 5 or 12 − 7.

Challenge

Let's play Tennis Sums!

Find a friend, then start by 'serving' to your friend with an addition or subtraction fact. They work out the answer quickly and return a fact back using the answer as the first number. You continue backwards and forwards until someone makes a mistake. The answers must not be above 20.

So a game could be like this:

    8 add 4 is ?   12 take away 3 is ?
   9 take away 6 is ?   3 add 12 is ?
        15… and so on.
         Have fun!

Brain Teaser

Write + or − in each circle to make these true.

1   7 ◯ 4 ◯ 3 = 14

2   9 ◯ 2 ◯ 8 = 15

3   6 ◯ 3 ◯ 4 = 5

4   8 ◯ 2 ◯ 4 = 2

5   11 ◯ 6 ◯ 3 = 14

Multiplication facts

Use this grid to help you learn the multiplication facts for 2×, 3×, 4×, 5×, 6× and 10×.

×	0	1	2	3	4	5	6	7	8	9	10
2	0	2	4	6	8	10	12	14	16	18	20
3	0	3	6	9	12	15	18	21	24	27	30
4	0	4	8	12	16	20	24	28	32	36	40
5	0	5	10	15	20	25	30	35	40	45	50
6	0	6	12	18	24	30	36	42	48	54	60
10	0	10	20	30	40	50	60	70	80	90	100

You can multiply in any order.

4 × 3 has the same answer as 3 × 4.

They both equal 12.

Exercise 1

Write different facts for each number.

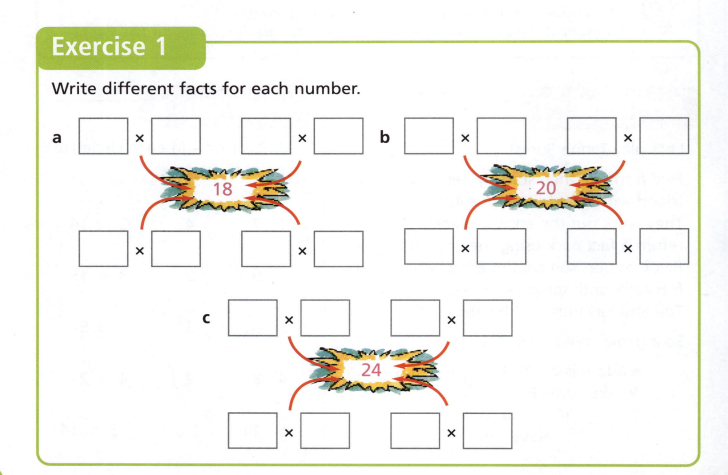

Exercise 2

Answer these as quickly as you can. Time yourself to find your quickest time.

a 7 × 2 =

4 × 4 =

5 × 9 =

3 × 8 =

6 × 6 =

4 × 3 =

b 8 × 3 =

9 × 2 =

5 × 5 =

6 × 7 =

10 × 4 =

4 × 9 =

c 7 × 9 =

5 × 8 =

6 × 3 =

4 × 7 =

9 × 8 =

5 × 6 =

Exercise 3

Complete each table.

Top Tip Use any facts you already know to help work out others quickly. For example:

If you know 5 x 3 = 15 then 6 x 3 is only 3 more ➔ 18. If you know that 4 x 4 = 16 then 8 x 4 is double 16 ➔ 32.

a IN ➔ × 3 ➔ OUT

IN	4		10		3
OUT		15		21	

b IN ➔ × 4 ➔ OUT

IN	2		7		5
OUT		32		16	

Challenge

Try this challenge.

Make cards for each of the facts for the 2x, 3x, 4x, 5x and 10x tables. Write the answers on the back of each card. Shuffle them and lay them in a pile face up. Set a timer and see how many facts you can answer correctly in 30 seconds. Check each answer as you go along. Keep a record of the number you get right and then after a few days see if you can beat your best score.

[2 x 6] [4 x 4]

Brain Teaser

Draw on the path that each number should take across the maze.

Each number can only land on a multiplication that has itself as the answer.

40 ➔	1×40	8×5	3×12	2×18	➔ home
24 ➔	2×12	4×9	2×20	4×10	➔ home
36 ➔	6×6	4×6	3×8	24×1	➔ home

Mental addition

Once you know your addition facts, you can use them to help work out harder sums.

Adding tens:

4 + 5 = 9

40 + 50 = 90

Adding on small numbers:

7 + 4 = 11

37 + 4 = 41

Using near-doubles:

8 + 8 = 16

80 + 82 = 162

There are lots of different ways to add 2-digit numbers.
Try these methods for 46 + 38:

40 + 30 = 70

6 + 8 = 14

70 + 14 = 84

46 + 30 = 76

76 + 8 = 84

38 is 2 less than 40

46 + 40 = 86

86 − 2 = 84

Exercise 1

Answer these.

a 40 + 30 = ☐

46 + 30 = ☐

b 50 + 60 = ☐

53 + 62 = ☐

c 20 + 70 = ☐

29 + 76 = ☐

d 40 + 80 = ☐

40 + 84 = ☐

e 60 + 30 = ☐

61 + 35 = ☐

f 80 + 50 = ☐

87 + 57 = ☐

g 70 + 40 = ☐

70 + 47 = ☐

h 30 + 80 = ☐

30 + 81 = ☐

i 70 + 60 = ☐

77 + 62 = ☐

Exercise 2

Add the rows and columns. Check the totals with the corner numbers.

a

19	24	
32	18	
		93

b

21	34	
26	17	
		98

c

15	31	
24	29	
		99

Exercise 3

Join pairs of numbers that total 100.

18

82

63   72   45   27

35

65

73   37   28   55

Top Tip Adding 19, 29, 39, 49 and so on, is easy because they are so close to a tens number.

34 + 29 is the same as
34 + 30 − 1 → 64 − 1 = 63

Challenge

Look at this magic square.

All the rows, columns and diagonals add up to the same amount.

4	3	8
9	5	1
2	7	6

Try finishing this magic square. It uses the numbers 1 to 16.

1			4
12			
	11		
13		3	16

Have a go at making up your own magic squares.

Brain Teaser

Answer these questions using the five numbers below.

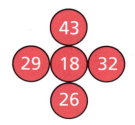

1   Which two numbers total 55?   _____

2   What is the smallest total that can be made by adding two numbers?   _____

3   What is the largest even total made by adding two numbers?   _____

4   Which three numbers total 90?   _____

Mental subtraction

There are lots of different ways to subtract 2-digit numbers. One of the best ways is to count on from the smaller number to the nearest ten.

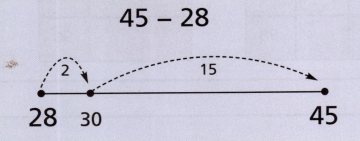

45 – 28

Count on from 28 to 30 and hold the 2 in your head.

30 on to 45 is 15.

15 add 2 is 17.

So the difference between 28 and 45 is 17

45 – 28 = 17.

Exercise 1

Use the number lines to help answer these. Count on to the nearest ten and draw the jumps.

a 36 – 17 = ☐

17   36

b 41 – 28 = ☐

28   41

c 44 – 19 = ☐

19   44

d 62 – 37 = ☐

37   62

e 53 – 26 = ☐

26   53

Exercise 2

Write the difference between these pairs of numbers.

a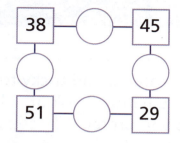

b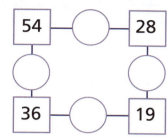

Top Tip Taking away 19, 29, 39, 49, and so on, is easy because they are so close to a tens number.

54 – 29 is the same as 54 – 30 then add 1.

Exercise 3

Write the missing number in each sum.

a 34 – ☐ = 19

b 52 – 13 = ☐

c 65 – ☐ = 25

d ☐ – 36 = 24

e ☐ – 47 = 17

f 83 – ☐ = 56

g ☐ – **48 = 92**

h 76 – ☐ = 28

Challenge

Here's a game to test how good your mental subtraction powers are.

Write down any 2-digit number, such as 62. Reverse the digits and write down that number ➜ 26.

Find the difference between the two numbers: 62 – 26 = 36

Add up the two digits from the answer: 3 + 6 = 9

Try doing the same thing with other digits and reverse subtractions. What do you notice?

Brain Teaser

Answer these questions using the five numbers.

a	b	c	d	e
41	27	32	19	25

1 Which two numbers have a difference of 7? ___ ___

2 What is a take away d? ___

3 Which number is 16 less than a? ___

4 a – c = d. True or false? ___

Written addition and subtraction

CALCULATING

Sometimes numbers for adding or taking away are just too big and tricky to work out in your head. That's when a pen and paper are handy! Look at these written methods and practise using the methods you prefer.

Addition:

$$78 + 64$$

```
   7 8
 + 6 4
   1 2   → 8 + 4
 1 3 0   → 70 + 60
 1 4 2
```

```
   7 8
 + 6 4
 1 4 2
   1
```

Subtraction:

$$94 - 67$$

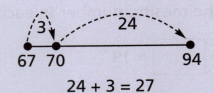

```
67  70              94
```

$$24 + 3 = 27$$

```
  8 1
  9̶ 4̶      94 is broken
 - 6 7     up into 80
   2 7     and 14
```

Exercise 1

Answer these.

a
```
    5 8
 +  3 7
 _____
```

b
```
  1 2 3
 +  5 9
 _____
```

c
```
    5 6
 +  3 7
 _____
```

d
```
  2 7 5
 +  5 6
 _____
```

e
```
    9 4
 +  4 1
 _____
```

f
```
  1 3 8
 +  4 2
 _____
```

g
```
    9 5
 +  7 9
 _____
```

h
```
  4 8 6
 +  2 4
 _____
```

Answers

PAGES 4–5

1 **a** 8cm   **b** 100   **c** 19
     d 45p   **e** 120   **f** 60

2 **a** £1.05 **b** 22   **c** 20
     d £1   **e** 30g

Brain teaser
     1 8   **2** 28   **3** 7

PAGES 6–7

1 **a** £1.22 **b** 65p **c** £2.12 **d** 23p

2 **a** 70p   **b** £1.10 **c** 95p
     d 25p   **e** £1.60 **f** £1.25

3 **a** £1.64
     b £13.65
     c £1.25
     d 75p
     e 20p 10p 50p 2p

Brain teaser
     1 £1, 20p, 10p, 5p, 1p coins
     2 £2, 50p, 10p, 5p, 2p coins
     3 50p, 20p, 20p, 2p, 2p coins
     4 £2, £1, 10p, 2p, 1p coins

PAGES 8–9

1 **a** 35 37 39   **d** 512 612 712
     b 72 70 68   **e** 56 46 36
     c 82 92 102   **f** 128 118 108

2 **a** 21 25 33   **b** 25 13 10
     c 16 31 36   **d** 50 34 30

3 **a** 137 138 139 140 141 142
     b 240 239 238 237 236 235
     c 809 810 811 812 813 814 815 816

Brain teaser
     1 -4 -3 -2 -1 0 1 2
     2 -3 -2 -1 0 1 2 3

PAGES 10–11

1 six hundred and ninety-four — 694
     six hundred and eighty — 680
     three hundred and sixty-eight — 368
     nine hundred and sixty-four — 964
     one hundred and twenty-four — 124
     six hundred and eighty-three — 683

2 **a** 90   **d** 700 + 30 + 4
     b 500 + 30 + 8 **e** 800 + 40 + 9
     c 700 + 40 +6   **f** 200 + 90 + 3

3 **a** 680 420 810 900
     b 32 40 74 68

Brain teaser
     1 20 90   **2** 30 60

PAGES 12–13

1 **a** 242 **b** 606 **c** 592 **d** 796

2 **a** Any number between 384 and 399.
        Any number between 399 and 406.
     b Any number smaller than 615.
        Any number between 615 and 637.
     c Any two numbers between 825 and 878,
        the first smaller than the second.

3 **a** 284ml 480ml 714ml 738ml 842ml
     b 560g 650g 681g 856g 865g

4 381 337 314 373 356
     300 — 400

Brain teaser
     1 219 216   **2** 370 374
     3 684 681

PAGES 14–15

1 **a** 50   **d** 80   **g** 60
     b 80   **e** 60   **h** 60
     c 10   **f** 50   **i** 40

2 **a** 300 **d** 300 **g** 500
     b 200 **e** 700 **h** 900
     c 200 **f** 600 **i** 200

3 27 42 58 74 85 96
     10 20 30 40 50 60 70 80 90 100

4 Any numbers between 350 and 449.

Brain teaser
     1 1400   **2** 3100   **3** 6200

PAGES 16–17

1 **a** $\frac{1}{2}$ **b** $\frac{1}{3}$ **c** $\frac{1}{5}$ **d** $\frac{1}{4}$

2 (shaded shapes)

3 **a** 3   **b** 3   **c** 4

4 Any 5 parts coloured red.
     Any 10 parts coloured blue.

Brain teaser
     1 $\frac{1}{2}$ **2** $\frac{3}{4}$ **3** $\frac{1}{3}$
     4 $\frac{9}{10}$ **5** $\frac{3}{10}$ **6** $\frac{5}{9}$

PAGES 18–19

1 a

+	4	6	2
7	11	13	9
3	7	9	5
8	12	14	10

b

+	6	3	11
5	11	8	16
9	15	12	20
4	10	7	15

c

+	6	4	5
12	18	16	17
14	20	18	19
9	15	13	14

2
a 5   b 3   c 3
d 7   e 7   f 6

3

a	b	c	d
9	13	3	9
8	15	2	8
10	11	5	8
10	13	7	6
7	13	4	9
7	11	4	7
9	16	5	4
9	15	1	9

Brain teaser

1 $7 + 4 + 3 = 14$ 4 $8 - 2 - 4 = 2$
2 $9 - 2 + 8 = 15$ 5 $11 + 6 - 3 = 14$
3 $6 + 3 - 4 = 5$

PAGES 20–21

1 a 2×9 9×2 → **18** ← 3×6 6×3

b 5×4 4×5 → **20** ← 2×10 10×2

c 6×4 4×6 → **24** ← 12×2 2×12

2
a $7 \times 2 = $ **14**   b $8 \times 3 = $ **24**   c $7 \times 9 = $ **63**

$4 \times 4 = $ **16** $9 \times 2 = $ **18** $5 \times 8 = $ **40**

$5 \times 9 = $ **45** $5 \times 5 = $ **25** $6 \times 3 = $ **18**

$3 \times 8 = $ **24** $6 \times 7 = $ **42** $4 \times 7 = $ **28**

$6 \times 6 = $ **36** $10 \times 4 = $ **40** $9 \times 8 = $ **72**

$4 \times 3 = $ **12** $4 \times 9 = $ **36** $5 \times 6 = $ **30**

3 a IN → ×3 → OUT

IN	4	5	10	7	3
OUT	12	15	30	21	9

b IN → ×4 → OUT

IN	2	8	7	4	5
OUT	8	32	28	16	20

Brain teaser

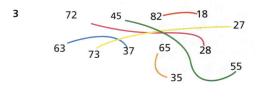

40 → 1×40   8×5   3×12   2×18 → home
24 → 2×12   4×9   2×20   4×10 → home
36 → 6×6   4×6   3×8   24×1 → home

PAGES 22–23

1
a 70, 76   d 120, 124   g 110, 117
b 110, 115   e 90, 96   h 110, 111
c 90, 105   f 130, 144   i 130, 139

2

19	24	43
32	18	50
51	42	93

21	34	55
26	17	43
47	51	98

15	31	46
24	29	53
39	60	99

3 72   45   82   18   27   63   73   37   65   28   55   35

Brain teaser

1 29 and 26   2 44
3 72   4 29, 43 and 18

PAGE 24–25

1
a 19   b 13   c 25
d 25   e 27

2 a 38 — 7 — 45   **b** 54 — 26 — 28
13   16   18   9
51 — 22 — 29   36 — 17 — 19

3
a 15   b 39   c 40   d 60
e 64   f 27   g 140   h 48

Brain teaser

1 32 and 25   2 22
3 25   4 false

PAGES 26–27

1
a 95   b 182   c 93   d 331
e 135   f 180   g 174   h 510

2
a 26   b 105   c 242
d 55   e 132   f 68

3

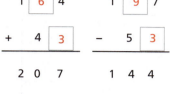

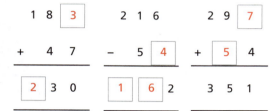

Brain teaser

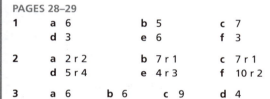

PAGES 28–29

1 a 6   b 5   c 7
   d 3   e 6   f 3

2 a 2 r 2   b 7 r 1   c 7 r 1
   d 5 r 4   e 4 r 3   f 10 r 2

3 a 6   b 6   c 9   d 4

Brain teaser

    2 groups of 15
    15 groups of 2
    3 groups of 10
    10 groups of 3
    5 groups of 6
    6 groups of 5

PAGES 30–31

1
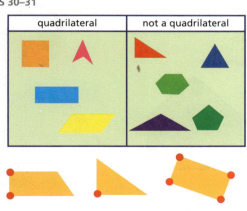

| quadrilateral | not a quadrilateral |

2
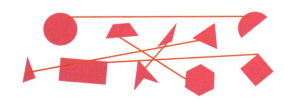

a trapezium   b triangle   c rectangle

3

Brain teaser

There are 30 triangles.

PAGES 32–33

1 a cuboids

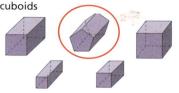

   b pyramids

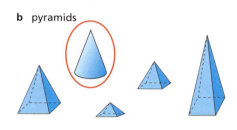

   c cylinders

   d cones

2 a False   b False   c True
   d False   e True

3

    3D-shapes

    c   f

        prisms   some
                      triangle
                      faces

        a e   g   b d

Brain Teaser

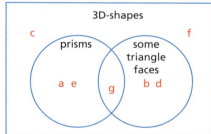

faces	5	6	7
edges	9	12	15
vertices	6	8	10

PAGES 34–35

1 a   b   c   d
   e   f   g   h

2 **a** 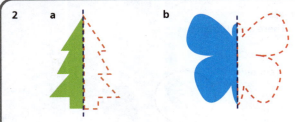 **b**

3 **a** **b** **c**

Brain teaser

4

PAGES 36–37

1 **a** East **d** North **g** South
b South **e** North **h** North
c West **f** West **i** North

2 **a** Bay 1 **b** Bay 4 **c** Bay 2 **d** Bay 3

Brain teaser

1 ✔

2 ✔

3 ✔

PAGES 38–39

1 **a** 4cm **b** 6.5cm **c** 4.9cm
d 7.6cm **e** 3.3cm **f** 6cm

2 **a** 300ml **b** 450ml **c** 350ml
d 150ml **e** 200ml

Brain teaser
Perimeter = 14cm

PAGES 40–41

1 **a** 3.10 **b** 7.30 **c** 6.40 **d** 11.15
e 1.55 **f** 4.45 **g** 12.05 **h** 9.20

2 **a** 15 minutes **b** 120 minutes
c 30 seconds **d** August

3 **a** 7.45 **b** 10.25 **c** 2.50 **d** 12.35

Brain teaser
The actual time for all the clocks is 3.55.

PAGES 42–43

1 **a** 55 **b** Javed **c** 45
d 85 **e** 25

2 **a** 40
b 2.40pm
c 10
d Any answer between 2 and 19.
e Any estimate between 123 and 147.

Brain teaser

House number	Black cat	ginger cat	white cat
1	Sam		
2			Jack
3		Ruth	

Test Practice

PAGES 44–49

1 9

2 Four hundred and one

3 4.45

4 6.15

5 pyramid (rectangular based)

6 45p

7 44

8 29

9 150cm

10 65 (reading across the rows:
25 + 40 = 65, 30 + 65 = 95, 35 + 40 = 75)

11
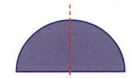

12 81

13 458

14 485

15 3.5kg

16 10p

17 pentagon

18

19 12

20 24

21 250ml

22 a and b

23 600

24 17

25 18, 21 and 27

Exercise 2

Answer these.

a
```
    8 3
  – 5 7
  ──────
```

b
```
  1 8 1
  –  7 6
  ──────
```

c
```
  3 0 4
  –  6 2
  ──────
```

 Top Tip *If you use a 'vertical' written method for adding or taking away, make sure you line up the columns carefully. Ones should be above ones, tens above tens and hundreds above hundreds. Written addition and subtraction is easier if you start with the ones column and work your way left.*

d
```
    9 4
  – 3 9
  ──────
```

e
```
  2 1 3
  –  8 1
  ──────
```

f
```
  1 5 8
  –  9 0
  ──────
```

Exercise 3

Answer these.

a
```
  ☐   7
+   3   8
─────────
    9   ☐
```

b
```
  ☐   6   5
+   ☐       9
─────────────
    4   2   4
```

c
```
  ☐   3   ☐
–       8   6
─────────────
        4   4
```

d
```
  1   ☐   4
+       4   ☐
─────────────
  2   0   7
```

e
```
  1   ☐   7
–       5   ☐
─────────────
  1   4   4
```

Challenge

Compare your written method with your mental method for adding or taking away. Use a mental method and then a written method for 58 + 37 and 64 – 36. Which was quicker? Are they similar methods? Can you explain your methods to someone else? Try the same thing with larger numbers.

Brain Teaser

The digits 1 to 7 are missing. Write them in the correct places.

```
  1   8   ☐
+     4   7
─────────────
  ☐   3   0
```

```
  2   1   6
–     5   ☐
─────────────
  ☐   ☐   2
```

```
  2   9   ☐
+     ☐   4
─────────────
  3   5   1
```

Division

4, 5 and 20 are a **trio**. They can make different multiplication and division facts.

$4 \times 5 = 20$	$5 \times 4 = 20$	$20 \div 5 = 4$	$20 \div 4 = 5$

This is useful for working out division facts.

$18 \div 3 = \boxed{}$ Change it to a multiplication fact.

$3 \times \boxed{} = 18$ The missing number is 6.

The division sign is ÷

Exercise 1

Answers these.

a How many twos in 12?

$12 \div 2 = \boxed{}$

b How many fours in 20?

$20 \div 4 = \boxed{}$

c How many tens in 70?

$70 \div 10 = \boxed{}$

d How many fives in 15?

$15 \div 5 = \boxed{}$

e How many threes in 18?

$18 \div 3 = \boxed{}$

f How many fours in 12?

$12 \div 4 = \boxed{}$

Exercise 2

Write the answers and remainders.

a $12 \div 5 = \boxed{}$ r $\boxed{}$

b $15 \div 2 = \boxed{}$ r $\boxed{}$

c $22 \div 3 = \boxed{}$ r $\boxed{}$

d $54 \div 10 = \boxed{}$ r $\boxed{}$

e $19 \div 4 = \boxed{}$ r $\boxed{}$

f $32 \div 3 = \boxed{}$ r $\boxed{}$

Exercise 3

Answer these problems. Check whether you need to round up or down.

a There are 28 children in a class. One table seats 5 children. How many tables are needed? ☐

b A farmer collects 38 eggs. An egg box holds 6 eggs. How many full egg boxes will there be? ☐

c Fred reads 4 pages a day. His book has 35 pages. How many days will he take to read the whole book? ☐

d A roll of material measures 14m. How many 3m lengths can be cut? ☐

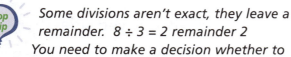 *Some divisions aren't exact, they leave a remainder. 8 ÷ 3 = 2 remainder 2 You need to make a decision whether to round up or round down for division problems. Examples:*
A tube holds 3 tennis balls. How many tubes are needed for 8 balls? 3 tubes are needed (one will have two tennis balls in it).
8 cakes are shared equally between 3 people. How many will each get? 2 cakes each, with 2 left over.

Challenge

Write each of the division facts for three times tables, choosing from ÷2, ÷3, ÷4, ÷5, ÷10, on 30 separate cards. Write the answers on the back of each card.

Shuffle them and lay them in a pile face up. Set a timer and see how many facts you can answer correctly in 30 seconds. Check each answer as you go along.

Keep a record of the number you get right and then after a few days see if you can beat your best score.

Brain Teaser

Class 4 has 30 children. The teacher wants to put the class into teams. How many different ways are there to divide the class into equal-sized teams?

2	groups of	15	children
☐	groups of	☐	children
☐	groups of	☐	children
☐	groups of	☐	children
☐	groups of	☐	children
☐	groups of	☐	children

2D shapes

A 2D shape is a flat shape. Look at the number of sides of each shape to help learn their names.

Triangle – 3 sides   Pentagon – 5 sides

Quadrilateral – 4 sides.   Hexagon – 6 sides

A circle, semi-circle and oval are shapes with curved sides.

Exercise 1

Sort these shapes. Draw them in the correct part of the Carroll diagram.

quadrilateral	not a quadrilateral

Exercise 2

Name these shapes. Draw a spot on each right angle.

a 　　　b 　　　c

_____　_____　_____

 Some shapes have right angles, which is a quarter of a whole turn.

For example, a rectangle has four right angles.

Exercise 3

Join each half shape to its matching full shape.

Challenge

Cut out a square and draw three straight lines at any angle across the square.

Cut along the lines and shuffle up the pieces.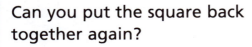

Can you put the square back together again?

Can you use any two pieces to make a triangle? Three pieces?

Can you make a pentagon?

Make different shapes with your pieces.

Brain Teaser

How many triangles can you see in this shape?

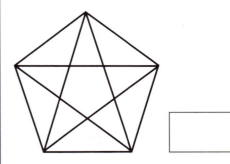

Be careful – some triangles can overlap.

3D shapes

A 3D shape is a solid shape.

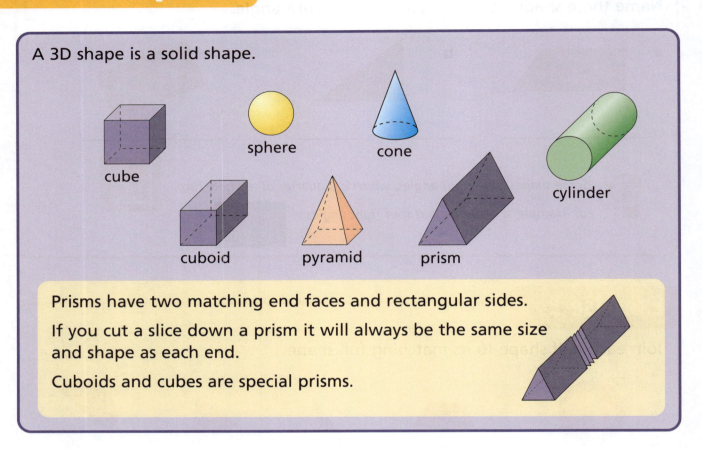

Prisms have two matching end faces and rectangular sides.

If you cut a slice down a prism it will always be the same size and shape as each end.

Cuboids and cubes are special prisms.

Exercise 1

Circle the odd one out in each set. Write the name of the shapes in each set.

a Name: _____

b Name: _____

c Name: _____

d Name: _____

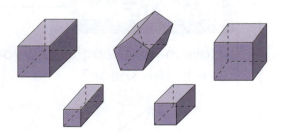

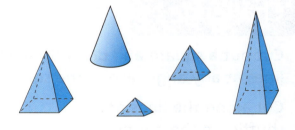

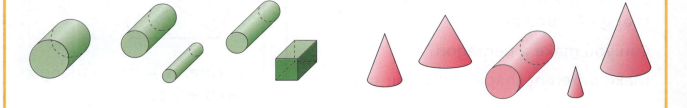

Exercise 2

Write true or false.

a A cuboid has a triangular face. _____

b A prism always has some rectangular or square faces. _____

c A sphere has no edges. _____

d A pyramid always has some rectangular or square faces. _____

e A pyramid has mainly triangular faces. _____

 Top Tip *There are three main parts to 3D shapes.*

This pyramid has 5 faces, 8 edges and 5 vertices.

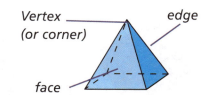

Vertex (or corner)   edge   face

Exercise 3

Sort these shapes. Write the shape letter in the correct part of the Venn diagram.

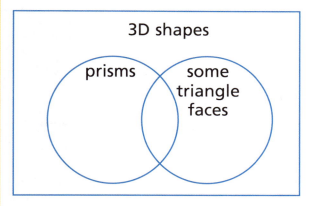

3D shapes

prisms   some triangle faces

a   **b**   **c**   **d**

e   **f**   **g**

Challenge

Next time you finish a cereal box, open it out carefully. Undo all the flaps and then lay it out flat. Sketch it onto a piece of paper.

Open up other boxes in the same way and draw them so they can be compared.

These are called 'nets'.

Brain Teaser

How many faces, edges and vertices do each of these prisms have?

faces			
edges			
vertices			

Reflective symmetry

A line of **symmetry** is like a mirror line.

One half of the shape looks like a reflection of the other half.

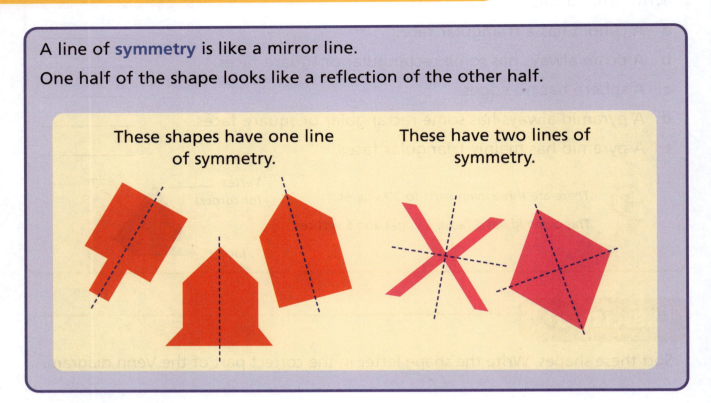

These shapes have one line of symmetry.

These have two lines of symmetry.

Exercise 1

Draw one line of symmetry on each shape.

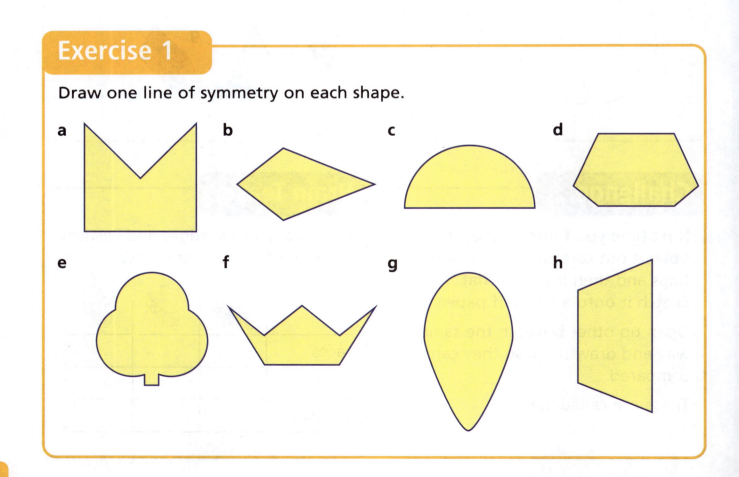

a   b   c   d

e   f   g   h

Exercise 2

Draw the reflection of each shape.

a

b

Exercise 3

Draw two lines of symmetry on these shapes.

a

b

c

Top Tip *Lines of symmetry are not always up and down or side to side. Sometimes they are sloping. Try testing some of the shapes on this page with a small mirror. Place it along the mirror line and the shape in the mirror should be the same as the shape behind it.*

Challenge

Fold a piece of paper in half. Cut out any shape along the fold line. Open out the shape and the fold line should be its line of symmetry.

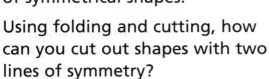

Try different cuts and make a display of symmetrical shapes.

Using folding and cutting, how can you cut out shapes with two lines of symmetry?

Brain Teaser

Which of these is a reflection of the first pattern? Tick the correct tile.

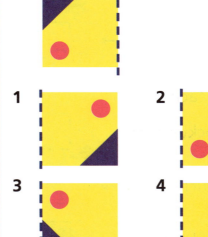

1

2

3

4

Directions and angles

Check that you know these:

Clockwise   Anticlockwise

Left   Right

Four compass directions

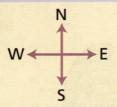

1 right-angle = $\frac{1}{4}$ turn

2 right-angles = $\frac{1}{2}$ turn

3 right-angles = $\frac{3}{4}$ turn

4 right-angles = 1 turn

Exercise 1

Which direction will you end up facing each time?

Always start facing North

a $\frac{1}{4}$ turn clockwise ➔

b $\frac{1}{2}$ turn anticlockwise ➔

c $\frac{1}{4}$ turn anticlockwise ➔

Always start facing West

g $\frac{1}{4}$ turn anticlockwise ➔

h $\frac{3}{4}$ turn anticlockwise ➔

i $\frac{1}{4}$ turn clockwise ➔

Always start facing East

d $\frac{3}{4}$ turn clockwise ➔

e $\frac{1}{4}$ turn anticlockwise ➔

f $\frac{1}{2}$ turn clockwise ➔

Top Tip

When you need to turn left or right, remember to face in the correct direction before turning. If you get in a muddle between lefts and rights try this:

Look at the back of your hands and stretch out your thumbs. The left hand looks like the letter L.

Exercise 2

Follow the routes. Where does each car park?

a forward 2 → turn right → forward 2 → turn left → forward 2 → turn left → forward 2 → turn right → forward 2 →   BAY [ ]

b forward 4 → turn right → forward 2 → turn left → forward 2 →   BAY [ ]

c forward 1 → turn left → forward 2 → turn right → forward 3 → turn right → forward 1 → turn left → forward 2 →   BAY [ ]

d forward 3 → turn left → forward 2 → turn left → forward 1 → turn left → forward 1 → turn left → forward 4 →   BAY [ ]

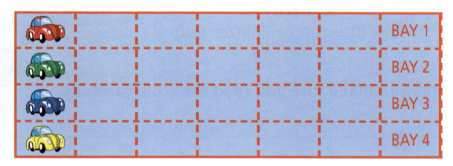

BAY 1
BAY 2
BAY 3
BAY 4

Challenge

Set up a mystery course in your classroom or home. Mark a starting point with an object, such as a chair, and use paces and turns to give someone directions to follow, to get back to the starting point.

For example:

START → 3 paces forward → quarter turn clockwise → 2 paces forward → three-quarter turn anti-clockwise → 4 paces forward → quarter turn clockwise → 2 paces forward → quarter turn clockwise → 1 pace forward → FINISH

Brain Teaser

Tick the right angle in each set.

1

2

3

Measurement

Try to learn these different units of measurement.

Length
1 metre (m) = 100 centimetres (cm)
1 kilometre (km) = 1000 metres (m)

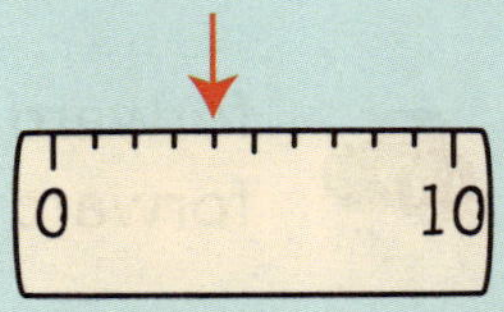

Weight
1 kilogram (kg) = 1000 grams (g)

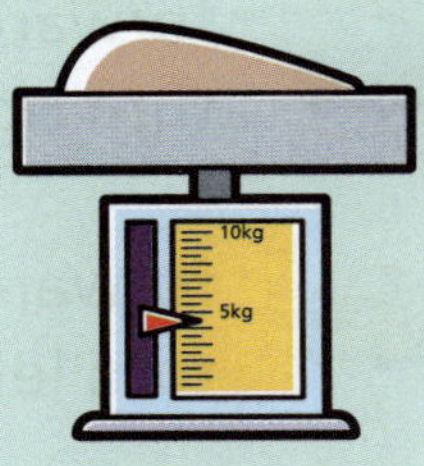

Capacity
1 litre (l) = 1000 millilitres (ml)

When you measure make sure you read the scale carefully.

Exercise 1

Use a ruler to measure these lines.

a _____ [ ] cm

b _____ [ ] cm

c _____ [ ] cm

d _____ [ ] cm

e _____ [ ] cm

f _____ [ ] cm

Exercise 2

Write the measures shown.

a
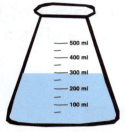

[ ] ml

b
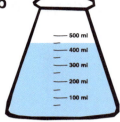

[ ] ml

c

[ ] ml

d
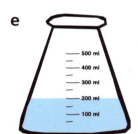

[ ] ml

e

[ ] ml

 Top Tip

Decimal points are used in measures and can be confusing, so look at them carefully.

3.5m = 3 metres 50cm = 350cm

3.05m = 3 metres 5cm = 305cm

The decimal point separates the whole unit from the fraction of the unit.

Challenge

Try playing this measuring game with a friend. Shout out a length, say 6cm. Now try and draw a line 6cm long – without a ruler. How close are you?

Give a point for every $\frac{1}{2}$ centimetre that you were away from 6cm – the lower the score, the better. Shout out five other lengths, draw, measure, then score. Keep a tally of your score.

You've done really well if you score below 5 points!

Brain Teaser

The perimeter is the distance all around the edge of a shape.

Estimate the perimeter of this rectangle.

Estimate = [ ] cm

Measure the perimeter.

Measure = [ ] cm

Reading the time

Clocks and watches use numbers or hands to show the time. To make it simple to read the time with any type of clock, read the hour first and then the minutes past the hour.

20 minutes past 7

Seven Twenty

35 minutes past 4

Four Thirty-five

Exercise 1

Write the times for these.

a

_____

b

_____

c

_____

d

_____

e

_____

f

_____

g

_____

h

_____

Exercise 2

Answer these time questions.

a How many minutes are there in a quarter of an hour? _____

b How many minutes are there in 2 hours? _____

c How many seconds are there in half a minute? _____

d Which month comes before September? _____

Try to learn these:

1 minute = 60 seconds

1 hour = 60 minutes

1 day = 24 hours

1 week = 7 days

1 year = 12 months
= 52 weeks
= 365 days

Exercise 3

Draw the missing minute hands on these clocks.

a 7.45

b 10.25

c 2.50

d 12.35

Challenge

Hickory, dickory, dock! Let's make a clock!

Make a 'tocker timer'.

1 Put blu-tac on a coffee jar lid.

2 Stick a card with the numbers of a clock onto blu-tac to make a 'face'.

3 Set the lid 'tocking' by setting it rolling.

Can you make the time go quicker, or slower?

Brain Teaser

In this Clockmaker's shop, all the clocks are telling the wrong time. Draw hands on the blank clock to show the real time.

20 minutes fast

50 minutes slow

25 minutes slow

Actual time:

Graphs and charts

Information can be shown in lots of different ways, using graphs, charts, tables and diagrams. With each type, read all the different parts carefully to understand it.

1 Read the title. What is the graph about?

2 Compare the bars. Read them across to work out the amounts.

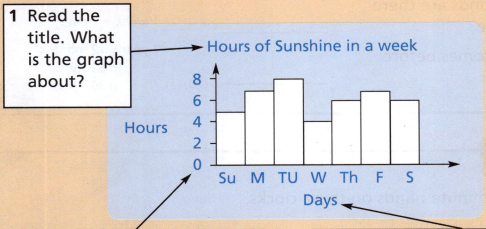

Hours of Sunshine in a week

Hours

Days

3 Work out the scale. Do the numbers go up in 1s, 2s, 5s, 10s…?

4 Look at the axis labels. These will explain the horizontal and vertical lines.

Exercise 1

Stickers collected by a group of children.

a How many stickers did Lara collect?

b Who collected 35 stickers?

c How many more stickers has Tom collected than Ali?

d How many stickers have Javed and Millie collected altogether?

e How many more stickers does Lara need to collect to have 80?

Stickers collected

Stickers collected

Children

Exercise 2

This pictogram shows the number of people on coaches at different times of the day.

coach times		
9.10am	🧍🧍🧍🧍	
11.20am	🧍🧍🧍	
1.30pm	🧍	
2.40pm	🧍🧍	
5.15pm	🧍🧍🧍🧍	

🧍 = 10 people

🧍 = less than 10 people

Top Tip

Pictograms are graphs made up from pictures. The important thing is to find out what each small picture stands for. Look at the key. For example, for this pictogram, one picture stands for 10 people. It means that some answers will be approximate. Half a person could be 3 or 9 – or any number less than 10.

a   How many people were on the 5.15pm coach?

b   Which coach had 17 people travelling on it?

c   How many more people were on the 9.10am coach than on the 5.15pm coach?

d   Approximately how many more people were on the 2.40pm coach than the 1.30pm coach?

e   Approximately how many people travelled on the coaches in total through the day?

Challenge

What's your favourite TV program? Carry out a survey of favourite types of TV programmes with your family, friends or at school.

You need to make up a list of types of programme for them to choose. Some examples to start you off are cartoons, news, sport, quiz…

Draw a graph or pictogram to show your results. Which is the most popular type? Which is the least popular?

Brain Teaser

 Sam

 Ruth

 Jack

My cat is black. My front door is not blue.

My cat is not white. My front door is yellow.

My cat is white. My front door is not red.

Write the children's names in the chart to show the information.

house number	black cat	ginger cat	white cat
1			
2			
3			

Test practice

TEST PRACTICE

score

1 What is the difference between these numbers?

17 8

2 Write 401 in words.

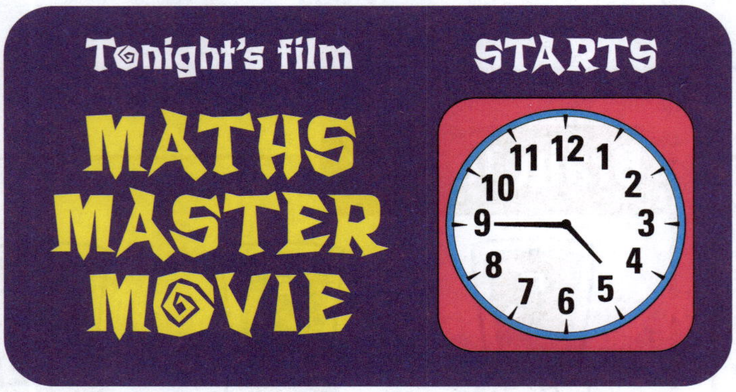

Tonight's film
MATHS MASTER MOVIE
STARTS

3 What time does the film start?

4 The film is on for 1 hour 30 minutes.
What time does it finish?

_____

5 Name this shape.

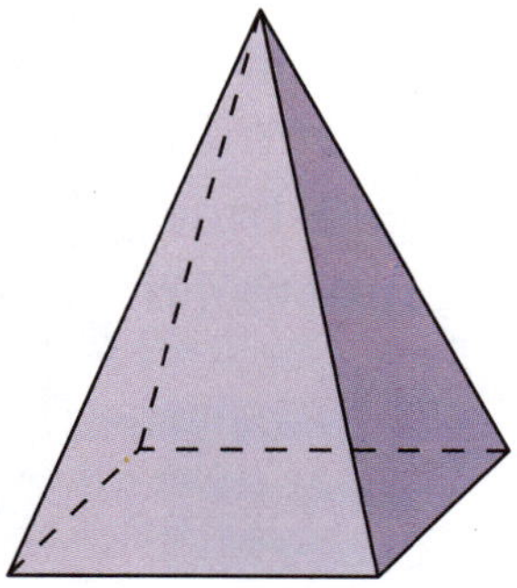

_____

6 A newspaper costs 55p. How much change will be given from £1?

_____

7 What is 19 more than 25?

_____

8 What is the next number in this sequence?

14   17   20   23   26   [   ]

9 What is 1.5m in centimetres?

_____

10 What is the missing number?

25	40	65
30		95
35	40	75

11 Draw a line of symmetry on the shape.

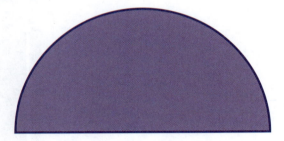

12 What is the next odd number after 79?

_____

13 Arrange these three digits to make the smallest possible number.

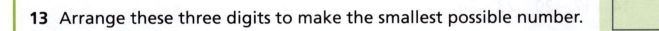

_____

14 Now arrange the digits to make a number as near as possible to 500.

_____

15 What is the weight of this parcel?

_____

16 Three drinks cost 30p each. What change will there be from £1?

_____

17 Name this 2D shape.

_____

18 Tick the right-angles on the shape.

19 What is half of 24?

_____

20 8 × 3 = ☐

21 How much is in this jug?

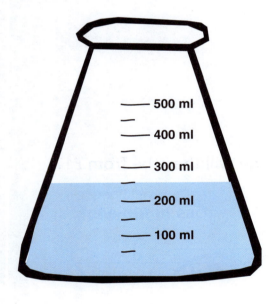

500 ml

400 ml

300 ml

200 ml

100 ml

_____

22 Tick the shapes that have $\frac{1}{4}$ shaded.

a   b   c   d

  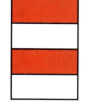

23 What number is the arrow pointing to?

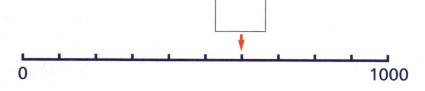

0   1000

24 35 − [ ] = 18

25 Circle the numbers that divide exactly by 3.

 22   18   26

21

16

27

Glossary

Carroll diagram a grid used to sort things into groups or sets

quadrilateral	not a quadrilateral

column a vertical line going up or down

19	24	
32	18	
		93

change the amount of money you are given back if you pay more than the price of an item. If £5 was given for an item costing £4.50, you would have 50p change

compare when you compare two objects or numbers you look for differences and similarities between them

decimal point used to show which digits are whole numbers and which are fractions. The digits to the left of the decimal point give the number of ones, tens and hundreds. The digits to the right of the decimal point give the number of tenths, hundredths, and so on.

With money, the decimal point separates the pounds from the pence

denominator is the number below the line in a fraction. It shows how many parts a whole shape or number of items is divided into.

e.g. $\frac{1}{4}$ of 12. The denominator is 4, so $\frac{1}{4}$ of 12 is 12 ÷ 4 = 3

difference the difference is the number you must count on to get from a smaller number to a bigger one. You can also work it out by subtracting the smaller one from the bigger one.

e.g. The difference between 4 and 9 is 5

digit is any of the ten numerals: 0, 1, 2, 3, 4, 5, 6, 7, 8 or 9. Numbers are made up from digits

fraction a number that is part of a whole number. They can be written in different ways: $\frac{1}{4}$, $\frac{3}{5}$ and 0.9 are all fractions. 0.9 is a decimal fraction

prism a solid shape with matching end shapes, such as triangles, squares or hexagons. The faces joining these end shapes are always rectangles

remainder if a number cannot be divided exactly by another number, it can leave a remainder or an amount left over. 11 divided by 2 is 5 with 1 as a remainder

row a horizontal line of objects or numbers going across

19	24	
32	18	
		93

rounding comparing a number to the nearest ten. A 'round number' is a number ending in zero: 10, 20, 30, 40, 50, 60, 70, 80, 90 or 100

sequence a list of numbers which usually have a pattern. They are often numbers written in order

symmetry when two halves of a shape or pattern are identical

trio a set of three items. A multiplication and division trio are a set of three numbers, such as 4, 5 and 20, that can make four facts:
4 × 5 = 20, 5 × 4 = 20, 20 ÷ 4 = 5, 20 ÷ 5 = 4.

Addition and subtraction trios work in the same way: 4, 6 and 10 are a trio: 4 + 6 = 10, 6 + 4 = 1 0, 10 − 6 = 4, 10 − 4 = 6

Venn diagram a way of showing how different things can be sorted into groups. The groups are known as sets

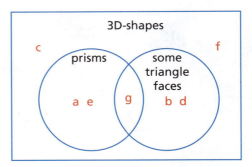